CREATING REMARKABLE LEADERS

SOLVING PROBLEMS AND MAKING DECISIONS

KEVIN EIKENBERRY

Pfeiffer
A Wiley Imprint
www.pfeiffer.com

Published by Pfeiffer
An Imprint of Wiley
989 Market Street, San Francisco, CA 94103-1741
www.pfeiffer.com

For additional copies/bulk purchases of this book in the U.S. please contact 800-274-4434.

Pfeiffer books and products are available through most bookstores. To contact Pfeiffer directly call our Customer Care Department within the U.S. at 800-274-4434, outside the U.S. at 317-572-3985, fax 317-572-4002, or visit www.pfeiffer.com.

Pfeiffer also publishes its books in a variety of electronic formats. Some content that appears in print may not be available in electronic books.

Participant Workbook ISBN 978-0-470-50192-4
Facilitator's Guide Set ISBN 978-0-470-50557-1

Acquiring Editor: Holly J. Allen
Assistant Editor: Lindsay Morton
Marketing Manager: Tolu Babalola
Director of Development: Kathleen Dolan Davies

Developmental Editor: Susan Rachmeler
Production Editor: Michael Kay
Manufacturing Supervisor: Becky Morgan

Printed in the United States of America
Printing 10 9 8 7 6 5 4 3 2 1

Contents

THE COMPETENCIES OF REMARKABLE LEADERS

The Remarkable Leadership workshop series is based on the book *Remarkable Leadership: Unleashing Your Leadership Potential One Skill at a Time* and consists of twelve workshops, based on thirteen leadership competencies from the book. (There is no workshop for the first competency, learn continually, as that competency is embedded in all the workshops.) Although you may not be attending the full series of workshops, all thirteen competencies are listed next.

Remarkable Leaders . . .

1. Learn Continually
2. Champion Change
3. Communicate Powerfully
4. Build Relationships
5. Develop Others
6. Focus on Customers
7. Influence with Impact
8. Think and Act Innovatively
9. Value Collaboration and Teamwork
10. **Solve Problems and Make Decisions**
11. Take Responsibility/Accountability
12. Manage Projects and Processes Successfully
13. Set Goals and Support Goal Setting

WORKSHOP OBJECTIVES

After completing this workshop, you will

- Understand the importance of asking questions to the decision-making process.
- Know the two main types of questions and how to apply them to a question-asking process.
- Understand a common problem-solving model.
- Know the pros and cons of four common decision-making approaches.

OPENING QUESTIONS

Ponder, and then write your answer:

1. What do I hope to gain from this session?

2. What do I think about (and how do I feel about) problems?

3. How does this impact my abilities as a problem solver and decision maker?

SELF-ASSESSMENT

Here is a quick assessment to help you think about how you solve problems and make decisions.

Use the following 1–7 scale on each question:

1 – Almost never	5 – Usually
2 – Rarely/Seldom	6 – Frequently
3 – Occasionally	7 – Almost always
4 – Sometimes	

I ask questions effectively.	___
I use questions to help develop a full understanding of a problem.	___
I think of questioning as a leadership skill.	___
I support the decisions others make.	___
I challenge people to try new approaches.	___
I consider a wide range of factors when making decisions.	___
I am willing to take calculated risks.	___
I use a proven problem-solving methodology.	___

ASKING QUESTIONS

Where does asking questions fit?

- With creativity?
- With coaching and mentoring?
- With learning?
- With influence?
- With focusing on the customer?

Why is it so important?

The Keys to Asking Great Questions

The keys to asking great questions are __________ and ___________________.

Two Types of Questions

Some Examples:

- 1a: Can you tell me how many people have signed up for the session today, please?
- 1b: Have you looked at the roster for the session today?

- 2a: Where all have you been today?
- 2b: Where have you been all day?

- 3a: What types of marketing approaches have you tried?
- 3b: Have you tried the new approach recommended by Dr. X in his latest book?

Open: Questions that encourage more than "yes" or "no" answers:

- Allows people to think about their responses
- Provides more than just facts, such as attitudes, emotions, and thoughts
- Creates an opportunity for people to share other relevant information
- Creates dialogue and partnership

Closed: Questions that can be answered with "yes/no" or other short responses:

- Brings conversation to a close
- Can be used to paraphrase as a check for understanding
- Good for gaining quick information in a hurry

A Question-Asking Process

1. Consider the purpose and intent of your question.

2. Consider the person you are asking.

3. Formulate your question.

4. Listen to the response.

5. Probe for more information if needed.

6. Be gracious.

7. Take action.

The Shewhart Cycle

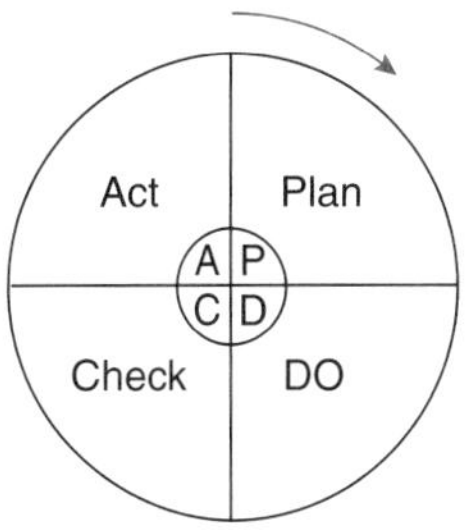

- Plan

- Do

- Check

- Act

Where do most people get stuck?

What do most people underutilize?

Plan/Do/Check/Act

Planning Step Considerations

During the planning step, you will

- Identify the problem using data.
- Seek to understand it from different perspectives (customers, suppliers, and other stakeholders of the work).
- **Clearly define the problem by writing a problem statement.**
- Identify the root causes of the problem by asking the Five Whys.
- Identify possible solutions.
- Select a solution to implement.

Do Step Considerations

Check Step Considerations

Act Step Considerations

DECISION-MAKING APPROACHES AND STRATEGIES

- Independent

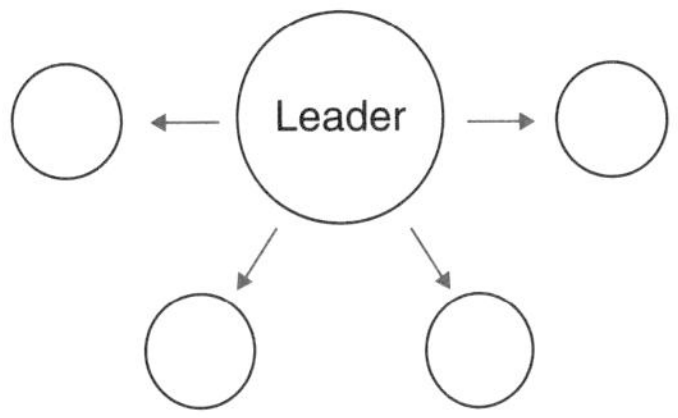

- Consultative

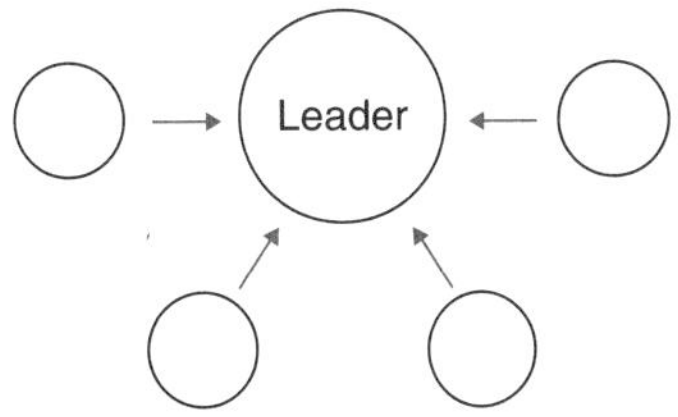

- Collaborative

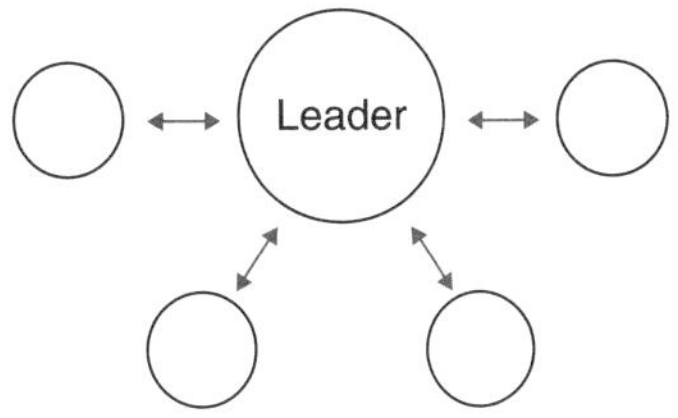

- Consensus

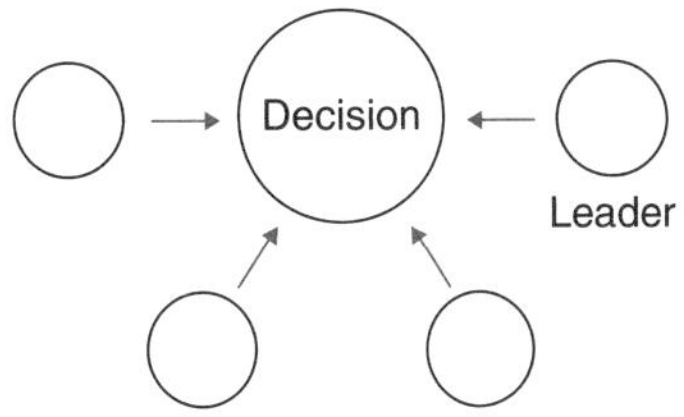

THE DECISION SLOPE

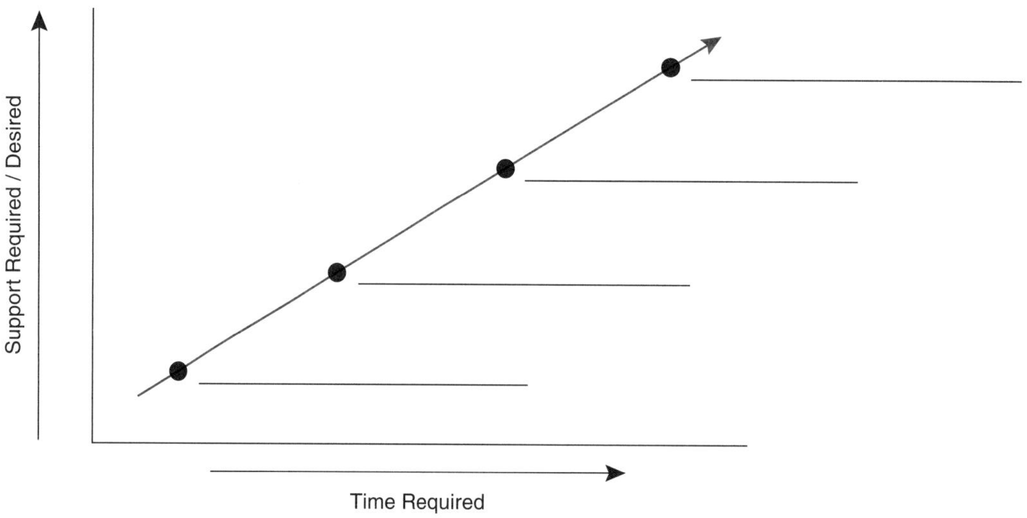

The implications?

The slope changer?

The big caveat?

YOUR NOW STEPS

Asking Questions

Rather than focusing these Now Steps on technique, consider your intent.

1. Think of a time when you realize your intent wasn't focused correctly, and reflect on your results.

2. Run back through the situation, and consider how you would have asked the question if your intent had been different, or if you would have even asked the question at all.

3. Make any notes and lessons learned in your journal.

Problem-Solving Basics

1. As you look at the work before you in the next few days, you will likely see at least one problem that you need to work on. Your Now Steps will help you work on solving that problem.

2. Identify the problem, and write your problem statement.

3. Don't do anything else related to solving this problem until you have written (not just thought about) this problem statement.

Decision-Making Approaches and Strategies

1. Look at a decision you need to make soon.

2. Make a conscious choice about how you want to make that decision.

3. Communicate that choice, and take the necessary steps to make the decision in that way.

YOUR NEXT STEPS

1. Think back to your goals for being here (page 2). Reflect on what you have learned that you can apply to your situation.

2. Teach a colleague (or your team) this content as a way to solidify your own knowledge and understanding.
3. Be responsible for applying these concepts and ideas in your work and the rest of your life.
4. Ask yourself: "Which Now Steps will I apply *right now*?"

5. Take that action!
6. Commit to your daily application to lock in your learning and achieve greater results!

"We move toward our potential when we turn learning into action."

~Kevin Eikenberry

ADDITIONAL RESOURCES

More problem-solving and decision-making tips are provided at **www.RLBonus.com.**

- For a tool to help you transform closed questions into open ones, use the keywords "open questions."
- For a list of tips to help you reach consensus decisions, use the keyword "consensus."
- For a tool to help you apply criteria to any decision, use the keyword "criteria."